Needle //
Shards

Other Books By EMP

#Beer
by Ezhno Martin

As I Watch You Fade
by James Benger

It's Too Late Now, Little Brother
by Mark Luke Seawood

Ten-Foot-Tall-And-Bulletproof
by Jason Ryberg

What Sits Between My Veins
by Samantha Slupski

Needle //
Shards

Poems by: Jeremiah Walton
+ Christopher Morgan

EMP
Kansas City, MO
http://www.empbooks.com

Copyright © 2017 by Christopher Morgan & Jeremiah Walton

All rights reserved. No part of this book may be reproduced, scanned, or distributed in any printed or electronic form, including information storage and retrieval systems, without permission. Please do not participate in or encourage piracy of copyrighted materials in violation of the author's rights. Please purchase only authorized editions.

First Edition

ISBN: 978-0-9985077-1-2

This book is a work of fiction. Names, characters, places, dates, and incidents are products of the author's imagination, or are used fictitiously, satirically, or as parody. Any resemblance to actual persons, living or dead, business establishments, events, or locales is entirely coincidental.

10 9 8 7 6 5 4 3 2 1

Design, Layout, and Cover Art: Christopher Morgan
Edits: Ezhno Martin

Table of Contents

Jeremiah Walton

What Happened To Your Finger?   / 1
Logic   / 3
Safety   / 6
Needle Eye   / 7
Norepinephrine   / 11
Satisfaction   / 14

Christopher Morgan

Fable Song   / 17
Seeing Red + Feeling Blue   / 20
The Long Poem   / 22
The Main Character   / 24
The Volta   / 25
Four Tanka   / 26

Jeremiah Walton *grew up round NH campfires in the shadows of rumbling freight. He's been off & on the road for ~4 years, running traveling bookstore Books & Shovels, performing from street corners to the NYC Poetry Festival + San Francisco Lit Crawl + Cleveland Snoetry Festival + Oakland Beast Crawl + This Lil Lit Fest Denver + Kansas City Poetry Throwdown. He's founder / co-manager of* Nostrovia! Press. *Raccoons + coyotes + rats are his companions.*

"What Happened To Your Finger?"

> *I want to separate,* Sid says

Her finger's broken

> *We're scratching an itch, wondering*
> *why it won't stop hurting.*

Her bike's brakes have needed changing for a while

How long has this been brewing?

> *Consciously? Today.*
> *After I left the hospital*
> *self-respect swarmed me*
> *Like—'holy shit*
> *my pinky is sacred*
> *my body is sacred!'*

> *I need to explore*
> *this physical with reverence*

> *I need to explore relationships*
> *between bodies*
> *outside sexuality.*

You are bringing romance to bodies
Chasing sexuality after fearing it.
I fear not having it
I fear bodies that aren't romantic.

There isn't a climax

an upheaval—

no slam
from a single event

Two people
who slid past,
a rockslide
to a mountain.

Logic

I don't remember every reason you explained about
getting back or *not getting back* then *getting back
but not back* & yo—

screw em both.

I'm exhausted
Writing nothing new
Editing you
Erasing me
living like projections
climbing out shadows
growing names

Alright, here we are

Here we go

both fearing the other person has a hidden partner
they're working with behind the scenes—workin
social experiments over the other—like

love me

love yourself

love me

love yourself

Fuck I don't want to show you this poem

12:56am
Sobriety is too bright

12:57am
Unscrew all the lights

12:58am

Oi—you're typing too fast
& self-referential again

Ah, well, fuck it—
keep flooding
out damns smoked dry
body lead by mouth
cut the line
loosen tongue
by the throat
spit on vulgarity
suck bigger toes
fuck someone else
dissect closure
get fronts together
breathe in deep
swindle cum of pleasure
sell out taste
safety-pin pierced
flip st peter
nail pinetree groans
routine insecurities
sift thru phoenix moans
monogamous melatonin
dreams death's dowry

self-loathing summits
love's thick pubes
& scheduled cuddles
& texas freight
& tequila gold
& rational miracles
& faithless hydration
& lonely—*oh*
for chrissake

12:59pm

How much of this is me,
how much of this is you?

                      All of it's you, ya idiot, Sid smiles

Safety

*What are some of the ways you curate
your actions to feel safe navigating being?*

*Any specific definition of safe
or is that meant to be loosely interpretable?*

*It's all so intertwined. I think keeping it general
is a good start? Like, I was going to say physically,
but headspace is physical & cerebral, etc, etc....*

*Take well lit busy car streets at night. Don't look
men in the eye, don't smile. Stay awake. Write.
Exercise/stay thin. Anything meditative. Think
of every possible way I am being exploited/
shamed/abused/enslaved/disrespected and come
up with an 'out' plan just in case. Keep my mom
nearby. Don't drink too much at a club. Don't show
bellybutton. Don't hitchhike. Don't ask for help.
Date men. Collapse my chest.
Limit attention to my tits.
Eat.*

Now your turn.

Needle Eye

I don't like how after sex you became more open,
                                                Sid says

It's not the sex, I say, *It's what it represents.*

                                        What's it represent?

I don't know—trust. I didn't expect it. I thought we were all done, ya know?

[S I D HOLDS A BAPTISMAL CANDLE OVER THE CAT WE'RE DISSECTING : A BLUE DOVE DRIPPING DOWN A GOLD GOBLET TOSSES GREEN & YELLOW SMOKE FROM ITS DESCENDING FLAME : WAX POOLS IN THE WOUNDS : HARDENS : PROMISES OUR SCALPEL STRUGGLE]

—unnamed hours parade by, ignored
by our not touching, talking
like moving thru St. Augustine's
spinal silence posture
widening the pew of christ's back
arched like a sunset
not touching the crucifix
nailed above alters laying odds
with prayers rolled from bodies
tearing desire out of chance
from untouched bass cranked
& gun-street girl hips
to dark chocolate muscle

      & coconut lipstick
from the way you walk
to my floral dress—all
stripteasing mask after mask
of mache comfort massaging
tense jaws as the cat's fascia
splits like 1000s of lil white fingers
letting go of Tucson rooftop uglies
      bumped over unwitting cops
of that tequila bottle you slung
      shattering like Flagstaff snow
swelling decisions shaved from a thesaurus writing
always crumbling memories stored unopened in
neural journals opening Albuquerque walmart
morning muscles shakin like spange cups to New
Orleans taking shots of motivation like oil to
lanterns, like

> *Jeremiah—I shouldn't have let you*
> *drive last night,*

to Alabama ice cream melting down our chins
like the sweetest sweat of night sneaking
thru a Miami art collective, slappin
moans against bathroom stalls, snatchin
beers & almonds for our Everglades bumble
touching an alligator & its translation
of our bodies as daily bread
baked on Sioux's seized engine
smoking white as thick web of mosquitos
wrap up itching like the swamp we escaped
thru to test the sun's patience
& moving on & on, to trailer park faces
rattled w/ relentless wrinkles, bored
w/ their lives the way we are,

them still storing Sioux like we're coming back,
coming back, to Miami, the self-capitol
where busking bloomed broke
& you wrestled history in cocaine's caves of sobriety
where Brendan & I slam life lines
like we're drowning, we're drowning
routine comfort bubbling to the surface
of wounds we didn't know were diving boards
like a candle to its puddle—like
Aye mom, we're kinda stuck in Florida,
swallowed for slowhond tickets to Kansas City,
Kansas City, good ol Kansas City, always
the Missouri side, where I fill an empty beer
w/ pennies & become Ezhno's salt-daddy,
where long walks grind knees loud w/ need
nourishing barbed wire round the body
> *Relationships are ego-based*, Sid says, *Full of
> demands—like assuming the moon's dialogue,*

Kansas City, where Ezhno's sugar momma
kicked down amtrack to Los Angeles,
Kansa City, where we made a solid five flying signs,
where police have better shit to deal with than us
& booze is cheaper than the easiest suicide —
continuing to breathe—
the fashion of this leather living
the fashion of investing labels, the cracks
on the tongue, the suckers
on the tentacles of
boyfriend girlfriend partner
warming that diddly darn ego
peeling heart-beat after heart-beat
till the bass learns to play for itself
& we go—go—go—get out—grow—go—

moving too fast to register—speedometer cracking
[CAN'T TELL IF IT'S THE WORLD SHAKING] an arbitrary whip **[OR MY HEART]** measuring love to the Bay **[CAN'T TELL IF MY BACK ACHES]**
where C.M. housed us **[OR —**

T O O   MUCH   T O O   MUCH
THIS WAVERING CANDLELIGHT
                         VISCERAL

    & BRIGHT]

thru shifting hues
you hop on top
& I bite your neck

we kiss & laugh
      how after a year

we still haven't figured out how to move
tongue thru the others' mouth

where's the line between romance & friendship?

Norepinephrine

This isn't you carving corners, right?
No—you wouldn't act like that, wouldn't
thin ice to whet independence—like
skidding first-class thru Hollywood's cracks
means confronting the attacker

You got more self-respect than that. . . right?

> *What good's worry doing you?* Sid says
> *You're only hurting yourself.*

Dammit, 'self-respect' isn't right
I'm not sure how to scratch this one

Dude, w/ all my on the road shit—
of course I'm gonna worry.

Sid—your logic makes sense
—external relationships
inhibit internal dialogue
       (depending on dosage?)

> *Then change your relationship w/ worry.*

Sid—your logic makes sense
—suspecting sex
mistrusting touch
   & instinct's butterflies
pinned to rigid spines
laced w/ muzzled muscles
ready for knife or glacier
ready for how you eat—what
you eat—what eats you

Hungry swells of synapses
program'what's processing you—'
to mean more than chemical
potential—electric mirrors
parroting fog & faces
assembling their view

> *I need to get out—I'm fucking tired*
> *of being mocked by potential threats.*

Sid—it's not be careful b/c you're a women
It's be careful b/c I love you

I don't know what to say that doesn't feel
controlling

Sid—your logic makes sense,
carving safety out the body men make target

> *When I get back*
> *I'm withdrawing to my head*
> *I'll still kiss you*
> *It'll just be alone.*

Sid—you're forging form
for whatever wings you damn please
& I respect it
& love it—you
digging past out
future's sky—bringing
in storms to steep
your scab collection—inhaling
where you want to go—exhaling
who you want to grow
Would you be dipping out
if you weren't in a relationship?

Sid stands, pupils
heaving light,
& slings a mug against the wall

Shards snap past my head

We stand silent—rolling
thoughts thru emotion's
stained sheets—too much
to give fresh blood to love
but dammit—here's a shot

at slowing enough to say *I love you*
     & you know it naked

at hearing your *I love you*
     & trust it true

> *All relationships are reflections glued*
> *together w/ projections of what*
> *you see they see in you,* Sid says
>   laying down among the glass

We'll need to give
these roosting lines
more than they hold--
fresh nests of glass
for the message each We carries

Satisfaction

This! This! You've found it!

After weeks of rummaging
you found enough motivation
to vomit in an alley
& cut lines you're satisfied with

Where's the next one?

Was it the trigger
or chemical?

Who's asking the question?

When does love not need an audience?

Christopher Morgan is a Lebanese American poet who grew up in Detroit, the Bible Belt of Georgia, and the San Francisco Bay Area, where he currently lives and co-manages Nostrovia! Press. *The Reviews Coordinator at* Alien Mouth, *and the author of two chapbooks, "Shadow Songs" (*Sad Spell Press *2015) and "Fables with Fangs" (*Ghost City Press *2016), he loves hiking in the redwoods and happy hour margaritas.*

Fable Song

1.
Carved from a fallen tree,
the walking stick
shatters a mace

2.
Slice the monster's head
and it regrows. Feed it
and it withers

3.
Much to everyone's astonishment,
the talking parrot reveals
it was magical all along

4.
The God wolf brings down
its mountainous paw,
cleaving a skyscraper

5.
After the eruption,
car-sized hornets returned
to their volcano nest,
carrying a woman and her child

6.
An astronaut discovers
his guiding star
was an abandoned satellite

7.
Having restored peace
to the hummingbird kingdom,
the bat with no shadow
flew back to the moon

8.
Each day, the angel
on the tiny planet
resisted dreaming
of cliffside promises

9.
An emotional robot
discovers fantastical beings
guarding a castle
inside the dying boy's heart

10.
Finding the never-ending avocado,
a former beggar fed his village

11.
Prisoners danced feverishly
while the eye remained shut,
only to fall silent when it opened

12.
After the last human died,
all together and all at once,
the birds of the world began to sing

13.
At the end of the forest-wrought trail,
a smiling blind bear asks wanderers

what they're afraid of
—to survive, say nothing at all

14.
Having a touch that turned
anything into flowers,
the boy finally found peace
in his self-imposed garden

Seeing Red + Feeling Blue

Dobermans chased him if he left home. The
Minotaur lunged from his fridge. Giant bird-eating
spiders crawled across his chest at night.

Then he ordered an official gun for mind-monsters.

Yet his psyche refused to relent: a high school bully
charging, a homeless man approaching, a crying
baby from a plane—these, too, wasted away with
grim satisfaction. A commercial about hair loss
mocked him from his television. Had he ever owned
a remote?

He shrugged, emptying another round at the
display.

Sparks flew, filling his room with smoke as he
coughed his way into the kitchen. Had he ever
owned a phone?

Trying the next best thing, he thrust the gun inside
his mouth.

Strangely, he couldn't get a dial tone.

*

Her favorite Collie in mid-leap. Her last dinner with
both parents. Being awake in a tiny dorm beside
an old lover—holding a frostbitten lantern, she
examined memories frozen within thick pillars of ice.

A tiny glacier of her father melted: he stood before
her, soaked, smiling, alive. She tried this time to
say something, but the water began to refreeze—he
vanished, white flakes spreading over his body like
a spider's wrapping of a fly.

She couldn't quite place it, but his frozen image
seemed diluted. Hadn't her father been smiling?
What about that scar, fracturing across his chin?

Must have always been that way, she sighed,
bringing her lantern to another frozen thought.

The Long Poem

your voice cracking
when you try to speak
is one of many signs
of the long poem;

when you take a hike
to find yourself, you're lost
in the long poem;

the long poem is a dragon
in the mountains, slowly
unraveling itself;

the long poem is an old boyfriend
that still texts you when he's lonely;

when you wipe your eyes,
you're already in the long poem;

opening chests in the attic
is an essential act
of the long poem;

the phrase, *all roads lead home*
is proof of the long poem;

the long poem is a glass museum
for your friends and enemies
stored inside for future viewings;

the long poem is a worn doorway
that your ex-husband is bashing
with his fists;

the long poem is the student,
the runaway, and the village,
all in one;

and how I come to you still,
unfazed, unloved, unsure—
this is the long poem

The Volta

the volta is the latch
being released
in a guillotine;

the drill instructor
demanding an about-face
was trained by the volta;

the volta notices the iceberg
in the distance, and steers
the ship for collision;

the volta
is rebellion;

a lover curdling her smile
at you mid-sentence
understands the volta;

the volta is a car
suspended mid-flip
like a penny on its side;

the volta looks upon a forest
and sets it on fire;

the volta carries you
into the clearing;

the volta denies
the past, then proceeds

The Main Character

your friend shoving you aside
to take your bullet is a sad perk
of being the main character;

the ruthless obstinacy to be
everyone at once can be found
in the main character;

the main character hides
in plain sight;

finding yourself transformed
into a monster when you wake
is a danger of the main character;

the main character can die,
only to return;

the sword in the stone
can only be pulled
by the main character;

the main character sits
on his bed, putting a pistol
to his head;

the main character leaves
home for long walks
at night and never comes back

Four Tanka

I.
I'm always knives-out
a chain of razors folded
behind each gesture
You who loves me: are you
paper? Or plywood? Or stone?

II.
I've learned to slow time
stretching this moment of you
taking aim at me
But what if I died like this,
motionless in your crosshairs?

III.
Woke in a sandbox
alone. Started digging for
you and never stopped
Each time I find your waving
hand, the sand pulls you deeper

IV.
The arrow you shot
into my chest has since grown
into a swan
This might be my final song
—I won't be bleeding long

ACKNOWLEDGEMENTS

Sincere thanks to the following places for first publishing these pieces:

- *Clade Song – "Seeing Red + Feeling Blue"*
- *Moloko House – "Four Tanka"*
- *TL;DR Magazine – "Fable Song"*
- *Yellow Chair Review – "The Long Poem"*

And big thanks to Ezhno + EMP for the love & support <3

www.ingramcontent.com/pod-product-compliance
Lightning Source LLC
Chambersburg PA
CBHW020627300426
44113CB00007B/794